D0857595

SMALL BUT *DEADLY*

DEADLY BACTERIA

By Greg Roza

Gareth Stevens
Publishing

Please visit our website, www.garethstevens.com. For a free color catalog of all our high-quality books, call toll free 1-800-542-2595 or fax 1-877-542-2596.

Library of Congress Cataloging-in-Publication Data

Roza, Greg.
Deadly bacteria / Greg Roza.
    p. cm.— (Small but deadly)
Includes index.
ISBN 978-1-4339-5728-4 (pbk.)
ISBN 978-1-4339-5729-1 (6-pack)
ISBN 978-1-4339-5726-0 (library binding)
1. Medical microbiology—Juvenile literature. I. Title.
QR46.R767 2011
616.9'041—dc22
                                        2010045995

First Edition

Published in 2012 by
Gareth Stevens Publishing
111 East 14th Street, Suite 349
New York, NY 10003

Copyright © 2012 Gareth Stevens Publishing

Designer: Michael J. Flynn
Editor: Greg Roza

Photo credits: Cover, pp. 1, (cover, back cover pp. 2–4, 7–8, 11–12, 15–16, 19–24 background texture), 5 (all), 6, 7 (all), 10 (all), 13 (bacteria), 17, 18, 20 Shutterstock.com; p. 9 Yale Joel/Time & Life Pictures/Getty Images; p. 13 (Great Plague) Edward Henry Corbould/The Bridgeman Art Library/Getty Images; p. 14 Guang Niu/Getty Images.

Printed in the United States of America

CPSIA compliance information: Batch #CS11GS: For further information contact Gareth Stevens, New York, New York at 1-800-542-2595.

CONTENTS

Words in the glossary appear in **bold** type the first time they are used in the text.

WHAT ARE BACTERIA?

Bacteria are very tiny **organisms**. We need a microscope to see them! Bacteria live just about everywhere in our world. You might be surprised to learn that they even live on and inside our bodies!

Most bacteria are harmless. In fact, many bacteria are helpful to people. For example, some bacteria that live in our bodies help us break down food. Others are used to make food and **medicine**. However, some bacteria can make us very sick. Others are deadly!

DEADLY DATA

The word "bacteria" means more than one of these organisms. A single one is a bacterium.

A microscope is a tool that uses lenses to make very small things—such as bacteria—look bigger.

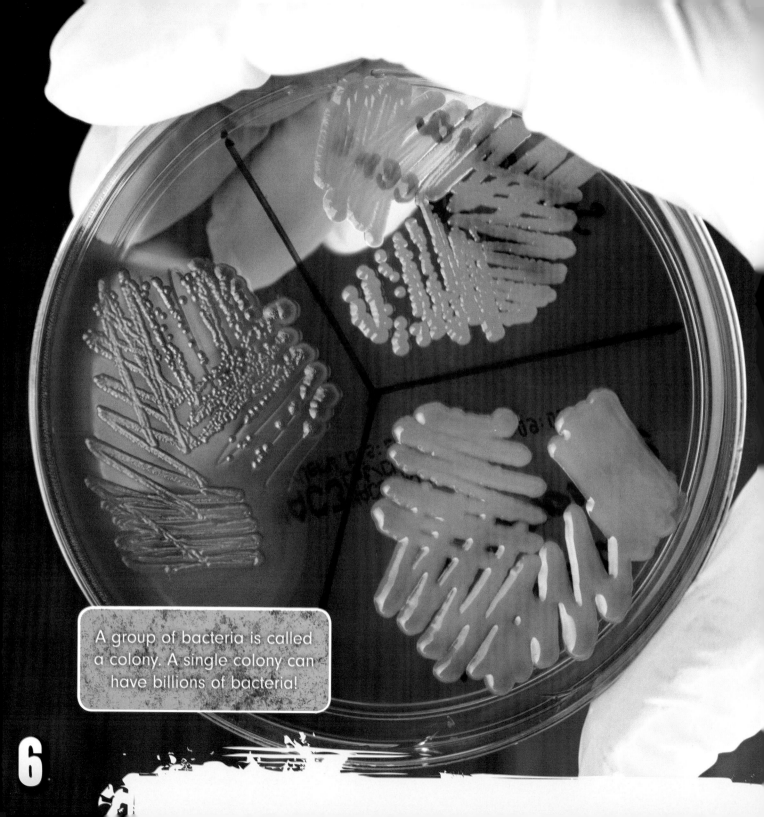

A group of bacteria is called a colony. A single colony can have billions of bacteria!

BACTERIA UP CLOSE

Bacteria are some of the oldest organisms on Earth. They are single-**celled** organisms. Some are round, and some are rod shaped. Others have a curled shape called a spiral. Some have hair-like parts on their surface that help them move.

These tiny living creatures multiply quickly to form colonies that have huge numbers of bacteria. Most bacteria multiply by splitting in half! A colony can double its size once every 10 minutes.

rod

spiral

round

ANTONIE VAN LEEUWENHOEK

Dutch scientist Antonie van Leeuwenhoek (LAY-vehn-hook) didn't invent the microscope, but he improved it. He built hundreds of microscopes during his life (1632–1723). Leeuwenhoek used his microscopes to see bacteria. He was the first person to clearly describe what bacteria looked like.

Leeuwenhoek's work led to many breakthroughs. Scientists discovered that bacteria cause some deadly diseases. This led to the creation of **vaccines** and **antibiotics**. It also showed the importance of hand washing to prevent illness.

DEADLY DATA

Bacteria are so small they are measured in micrometers. One micrometer is one-millionth (0.000001) of a meter!

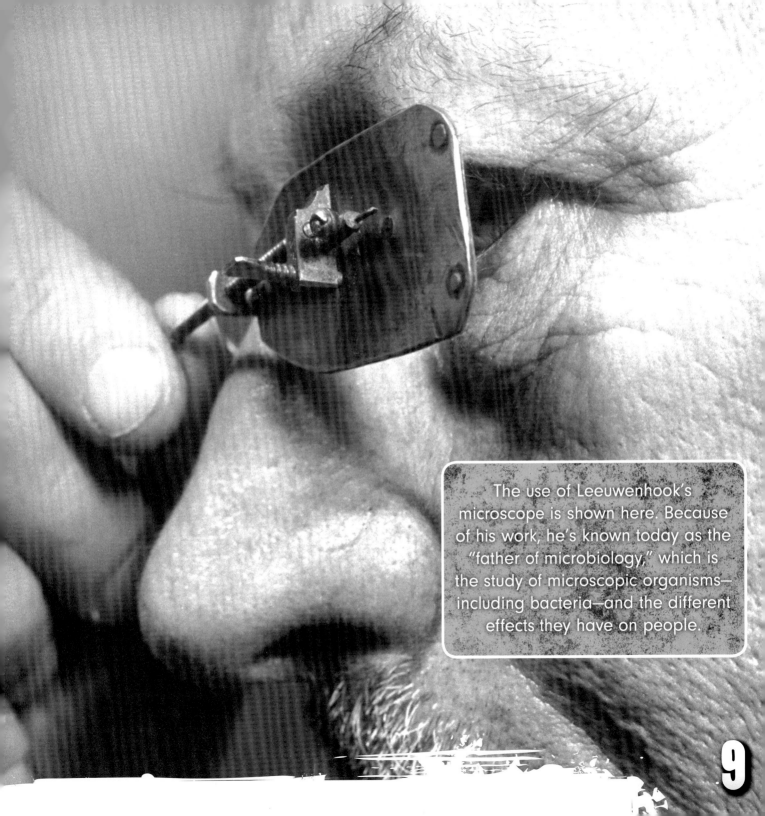

The use of Leeuwenhook's microscope is shown here. Because of his work, he's known today as the "father of microbiology," which is the study of microscopic organisms—including bacteria—and the different effects they have on people.

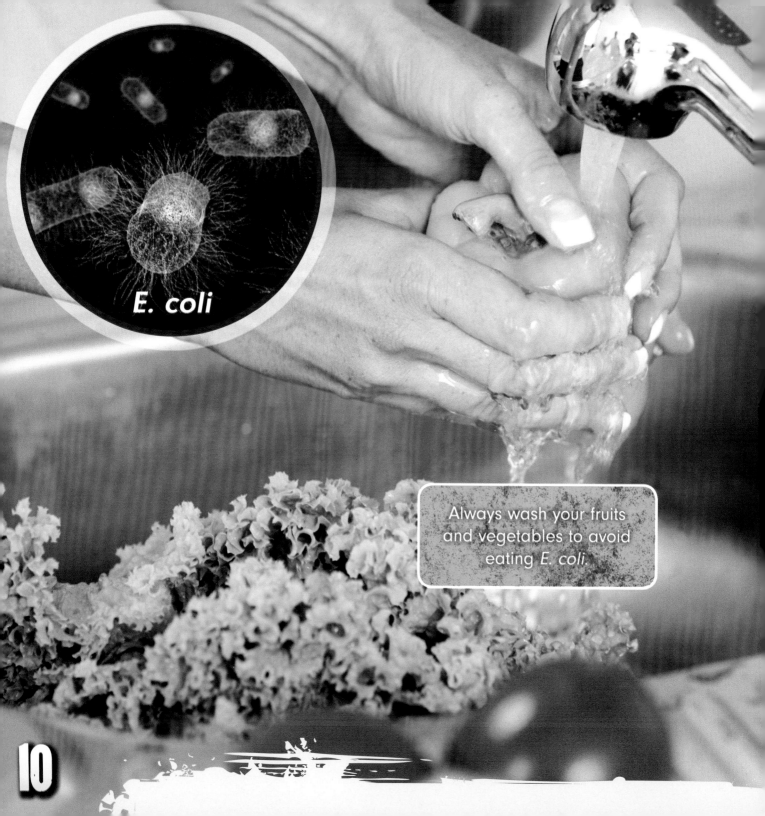

E. coli

Always wash your fruits and vegetables to avoid eating *E. coli.*

HARMFUL BACTERIA

Harmful bacteria cause sickness when they enter people's bodies. This can happen when a sick person sneezes and you breathe it in. Or it can happen when you touch something a sick person touched. We often call harmful bacteria "germs."

Have you ever had food poisoning? Most cases of food poisoning are caused by eating food that contains harmful bacteria. You may have heard of a bacteria called *E. coli*. Some types of *E. coli* cause food poisoning that can be deadly.

DEADLY DATA

Lyme disease is a bacterial illness that can be caught from a bug called a tick. Without proper treatment, it can be deadly.

THE PLAGUE

During the 1300s, between one-quarter and one-third of the people in Europe died of plague. People got plague from a harmful bacteria that lived in fleas found on rats and mice. One bite from a "rat flea" was enough to spread the disease. Plague caused many **symptoms**, including fever, chills, painful bumps, blackening of the fingers and toes, and stomach pain. It commonly caused death.

Plague still exists today. However, thanks to antibiotics, it's far less deadly.

DEADLY DATA

In the 1300s, plague was also called the "Black Death."

plague
bacteria

Plague struck London in 1665.
Historians believe it may have killed
more than 75,000 people. Many of the
dead were buried in mass graves.

13

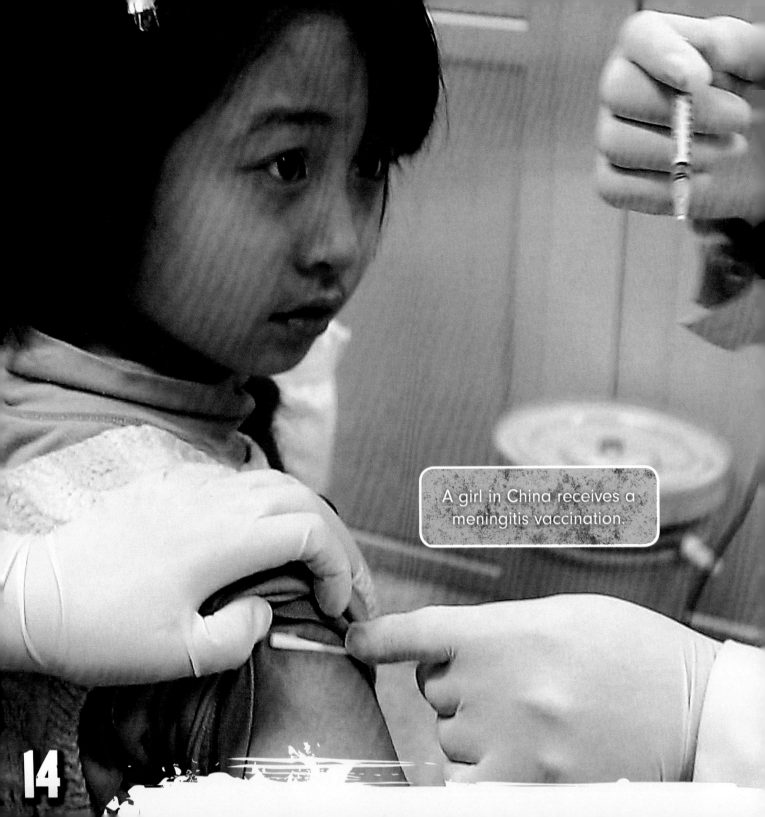

A girl in China receives a meningitis vaccination.

BACTERIAL MENINGITIS

Meningitis (meh-nuhn-JY-tuhs) is a swelling of the **membranes** around the brain. Many things can cause meningitis, but meningitis caused by bacteria carries the most danger. It most often strikes babies and small children.

A bacterial **infection** in a person's body can be carried by the blood to the membranes around the brain. As the bacteria multiply, the membranes become swollen. Symptoms include a bad headache, throwing up, and a stiff neck. Bacterial meningitis can lead to death in just hours.

TUBERCULOSIS

Tuberculosis, or TB, is an illness that usually involves the lungs. However, it can also involve other parts of the body. It's caused by a harmful bacteria. TB is spread when someone with the disease in their lungs coughs or sneezes. Others can get TB by breathing in the germs.

Symptoms of TB in the lungs include fever, chills, coughing, chest pain, weakness, and weight loss. TB was once the leading cause of death in the United States.

DEADLY DATA

Many famous people have died of TB, including First Lady Eleanor Roosevelt and baseball player Christy Mathewson.

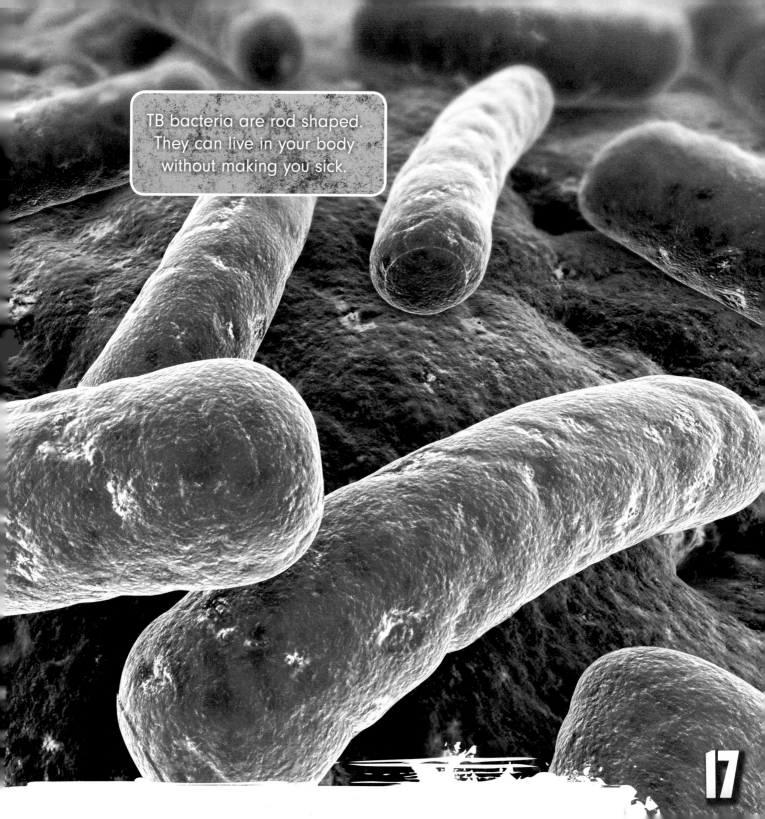

TB bacteria are rod shaped. They can live in your body without making you sick.

Cooking food is the best way to kill cholera bacteria. It's not a good idea to eat raw vegetables in a place where cholera is common.

CHOLERA

Cholera is an infection of the small intestine. It's caused by food and water that contain a harmful bacteria. Cholera symptoms include fever, stomach pain, throwing up, and **diarrhea**. Someone who has cholera can lose a lot of water quickly. Without proper treatment, cholera can lead to death.

Cholera first appeared in part of India called Bengal in the early 1800s. It spread across the country, and then the rest of the world. Each year, more than 100,000 people die of cholera.

STAYING SAFE

Thanks to antibiotics and vaccines, bacterial diseases are far less common today than they were in the past. Still, it's important to know how to avoid getting a bacterial disease.

Always wash your hands after using the bathroom and before and after preparing food. Always cover your mouth with your arm or a tissue when you cough or sneeze. If you're traveling to a country where bacterial diseases are common, use bottled water for drinking and even brushing your teeth.

ILLNESS AND SYMPTOMS

Bacterial Illness	Symptoms
food poisoning	stomach pain, throwing up, diarrhea
Lyme disease	chills, fever, headache, tiredness, muscle pain, itching, stiff neck
plague	fever, chills, painful bumps, blackening of the fingers and toes, stomach pain
bacterial meningitis	bad headache, throwing up, stiff neck
tuberculosis	fever, chills, coughing, chest pain, weakness, weight loss
cholera	fever, stomach pain, throwing up, diarrhea

GLOSSARY

antibiotic: a drug that can kill germs, including harmful bacteria

cell: the smallest basic part of a living thing

diarrhea: very soft or runny solid waste from a person or animal

infection: a sickness caused by germs

medicine: a drug taken to make a sick person well

membrane: a soft, thin layer of living matter

organism: a living thing

symptom: a sign that shows someone is sick

vaccine: a shot that keeps a person from getting a certain sickness

FOR MORE INFORMATION

BOOKS

Biskup, Agnieszka. *The Surprising World of Bacteria with Max Axiom, Super Scientist.* Mankato, MN: Capstone Press, 2010.

Parker, Steve. *Cocci, Spirilla & Other Bacteria.* Minneapolis, MN: Compass Point Books, 2009.

WEBSITES

ilovebacteria.com
ilovebacteria.com
Read more about bacteria, as well as other science topics.

Quiz Your Noodle! Bacteria
kids.nationalgeographic.com/kids/games/puzzlesquizzes/quizyournoodle-bacteria/
Take a quiz about bacteria.

INDEX